Author

Sergio Coltellacci

Translated by M. Antonietta Mejia

Principles to succeed

in the wonderful world of sales

"OUR GREATEST WEAKNESS LIES IN GIVING UP. THE MOST CERTAIN WAY TO SUCCEED IS ALWAYS TO TRY JUST ONE MORE TIME." - Thomas Edison.

"SETTING GOALS IS THE FIRST STEP IN TURNING THE INVISIBLE INTO THE VISIBLE." - Tony Robbins.

"THE HARDER THE CONFLICT, THE MORE GLORIOUS THE TRIUMPH." - Thomas Paine.

"WE HERD SHEEP, WE DRIVE CATTLE, WE LEAD PEOPLE. LEAD ME, FOLLOW ME, OR GET OUT OF MY WAY." - George S. Patton.

"THERE IS ALWAYS ROOM AT THE TOP." - Daniel Webster.

"A GOAL IS A DREAM WITH A DEADLINE." - Napoleon Hill.

To all of the champions that have followed me throughout the years, and that have allowed me to professionalize in the world of direct and creative sales.

REVIEWS BY OUR READERS

"The book Positive Mental Attitude by Sergio Coltellacci, is unlike any other motivational book I've ever read. After 5 years of not working and giving my mind limits of what and what I can't do, I got up the next day and started my next steps to be successful in my future. It had changed my whole mind set. I truly would recommend this book to anyone. Any part of your life your struggling in, wether it be motivation, or thinking you can't do something, this book will push you to open you mind and know it's you who is stopping you from succeeding"

Christa Suárez - Real State Agent and Mortgage Broker

"This book offers a daily help. I have put into practice each chapter and I see the results in my life it really helped me to change my attitude, I was able to became more organize accountable and helped me to achieve discipline. The results are evident in my personal life and work. With my new positive mental attitude, we have better results in the whole team. I want to thanks the author for this book"

Esperanza Ariza - Property manager

"This book captivates the realization of how you can adapt positive thoughts in any circumstance. It inspires me to have a positive mindset that leads me to succeed every day"

Dr. Dianexy Falcon

"I would have never imagined that a book would teach me the importance of wellbeing to sell... this is a great book "

Pablo Azar – Empresario, Pintor y Actor

"This book allowed to do a self assesment of my capabilities as a leader. I was able to identify which areas I need to work on to improve my leadership skills."

Ana C. Grajales – Empresaria, Actriz y Creadora de Contenido

CONTENT

Prologue by Arianna Coltellacci   pg. 6

Introduction   pg. 10

Part I- The sales profession   pág. 17

Part II – Advisor profile   pág. 32

Part III - Sales process   pág. 56

Part IV - The Art of Selling   pág. 66

Part V - Professional Ethics   pág. 75

Part VI - The Power of Trust   pág. 81

Part VII - The Power of Motivation   pág. 87

Part VIII - The Power of Goals   pág. 93

Part IX - The Power of Enthusiasm   pág. 101

Part X - The Power of Success   pág. 107

Part XI - The Power of Leadership   pág. 120

Part XII - In Search of Excellence   pág. 151

Part XIII - The Successful Advisor   pág. 162

PROLOGUE

By Arianna Coltellaci

When I heard the title of Sergio Coltelacci's second book, "The Fantabulous World of Sales", author to the already known "Positive Mental Attitude=Success", I could not avoid reminiscing about my childhood memories and each and every one of the different stages I experienced as a grew up.

Mysteriously, I found myself sitting in the university back in 1999, where I received my marketing and publishing degree and, all I could think of was that I had achieved my goal of finishing my studies and was finally prepared to go out into the real world. I rapidly found a job as a creative copywriter for a very important publishing company in Caracas, Venezuela, place where I was born and raised.

However, as big as my name appeared on my degree, my future seemed to be doomed to being an employee for life, in a company where I was just another number, with a basic, let's say mediocre salary and, to top it all off, my vacations were not only limited but would depend on the agency's needs. After having put so much time and effort into my studies, my future didn't seem like a very promising one. I wasn't very passionate with the idea of seeing the end of my life's movie, where I would be able to fully enjoy it if I was able to reach my retirement. It was truly depressing.

Despite all of what I have related, one day, influenced by the author of this book, Sergio Coltelacci, I decided to make my entry into "The Fantabulous World of Sales" and pursue what would become a very promising and satisfactory career. I can't hide the passion I feel as I read and share this book with you and I realized at my 47 years of age, that I know nothing more, nothing better, than to sell.

This book is a confirmation that the decision I made to dedicate my life so vehemently to this career was the best choice I could have ever taken. It demands a daily preparation-mentally, physically and spiritually- where the personal and financial compensations are unlimited. In this particular book, I found all of the ingredients to strengthen, nurture and fine-tune my career as a salesperson. I am currently involved in direct sales, both on a personal or group basis, of an important international time sharing company with their main headquarters in the United States.

With the guidance of this book, I was able to take my career to a higher level and, it will give you the tools to becoming a winner in the world's most competitive career. As a result of what I have learned and applied from this book's invaluable advice, in many occasions, I have reached the first 5 places in my office, accomplishing personal and economical goals that as an employee, would have been impossible to attain. Most importantly, my job consists in helping my clients fill their needs through our services and products.

Remember, if you are going to do something, do your best, put in 100%, be number 1 in your company. Congratulations! If you are reading this book, you have made the best investment in your career. Once you have finished reading it, you will experience an internal and external change that will help you grow in leadership through "The Fantabulous World of Sales".

INTRODUCTION

You may wonder why I have used the term - also non-existent -, **FANTABULOUS**, this is the synthesis of two adjectives, **FANTASTIC and FABULOUS**, which represent what truly represents the oldest profession in the world: **DIRECT OR CREATIVE SALES.**

It is an honor and a privilege to be a direct or creative salesperson.

The great motivator and writer of many books on self-improvement Zig Ziglar is absolutely right when he emphatically stated, "YOUR ATTITUDE, NOT YOUR APTITUDE, WILL DETERMINE YOUR ALTITUDE."

Indeed, a salesperson is not someone who convinces people to sell their product, on the contrary, they must, with a lot of Positive Mental Attitude, paint the ideal picture for the customer to buy. Also, they must be tactful and understand the customer's needs. They must be a person who knows what they are looking for, having simple, clear goals, and making all the necessary efforts to achieve them. Their greatest virtue is constancy; they will always advise their clients to make the right decisions when they purchase the product or service that they distribute. They should be concerned about leading a healthy lifestyle, not smoking or drinking excessively, doing a little exercise, and should also be thrifty, but at the same time realistic, that is, living the momento fully. For all these reasons and more, the salesperson is a very, very important individual in modern society.

Unfortunately, many people believe that the sales profession is the last link in society, where only those who do not know how to do anything turn, thinking that it is easy to do it. Indeed, a majority start selling as a way out of their situation and have a good excuse to justify their economic situation, blaming the difficulties that exist in each country. To achieve the success you seek, you must think that **destiny is not based on luck but on determination.**

Sadly, we do not want to acknowledge that since we are born, we are all salespeople. Mothers immediately recognize what their newborn needs by the way they cry, professionals sell their knowledge, workers sell their skills, artists sell their creations, etc. In fact, we are all, inadvertently, salespeople. In the process of practicing our activity, our confidence will grow and with it, the faith and enthusiasm to finally have a Positive Mental Attitude that will set our progress in life.

The salesperson or advisor who wants to achieve success must, like any professional, constantly prepare and specialize themselves. Sadly, why do most newcomers fail without being able to enjoy the great opportunities that this wonderful profession generously provides for all? There are many reasons why they do not achieve the desired success. The most important are: the fear of failure due to lack of confidence in their abilities, not setting real goals and not dedicating all the energy to their achievement. That is why, when faced with the first obstacle, they abandon it. In contrast, the professional salesperson knows that obstacles are those dreadful things that are seen when their eyes are taken off their goals. They do not worry about what others think, say or do, and as someone said: **"you must dare to dream to go where you please and be what you want to be."** Remember, no one is going to solve your problems. You, and only you, are the architect of all the good and bad that happens to you.

If people would only change their Mental Attitude and think like Orison Swett Marden (1850-1924) American writer and pioneer of self-help books, **Achievement Is Not Always Success, While**

Reputed Failure Often Is. Or what Henry Ford (1863-1947), the greatest automobile manufacturer, inventor of modern production lines used for mass production used to say: **"THOSE WHO QUIT ARE MORE NUMEROUS THAN THOSE WHO FAIL."**

Unfortunately, many salespeople do not realize the great opportunities that this generous profession offers, due to their lack of confidence, they do not understand them. We must learn from the Dai-Sensei Morihei Ueshiba (1883-1968), the famous master of Japanese martial art -creator of the discipline of Aikido and considered one of the best Dai-Sensei-, when he stated:" **FAILURE IS THE KEY TO SUCCESS, EACH MISTAKE TEACHES US SOMETHING."** We are the result of all of our successes and failures. It is precisely what happens throughout our lives which forge our confidence and transform us into better Advisors, reducing or eliminating the fear of failure.

Finally, another cause of the failure of many would-be Salespeople is leadership that falls short of motivating all of these individuals who embrace the sales profession with hope.

Many of the Leaders confuse motivation with manipulation. The meaning of Motivation according to our dictionary is:" **GIVE CAUSE OR REASON. EXPLAIN THE REASONS WHY SOMETHING HAS BEEN DONE OR WHY SOMETHING SHOULD BE DONE."** Instead, manipulation according to our dictionary means: "**INFLUENCE OTHERS WITH SKILLFUL AND DECEPTIVE MEANS, TO SERVE ONES OWN INTERESTS."**

Regrettably, many Leaders use manipulation to achieve their own interests without caring about the future of the members of their organizations. The big companies are to blame also. These should be concerned with training their leadership to learn the art of motivation, starting with their managers, teaching by example.

I would like to close with the following phrase from Og Mandino, one of the world's leading specialists in motivational books: **"ALWAYS DO YOUR BEST. WHAT YOU PLANT NOW, YOU WILL HARVEST LATER."**

FIRST PART

THE SALES PROFESSION

"Everything you've ever wanted is on the other side of fear."

Jeffrey Gitomer

Many years ago I was fascinated by hunting, although today I consider it a cruel and unjustifiable act, and on one occasion I was with a friend hunting in Italy. It was very hot and we were both walking in a vast plain when unexpectedly a cow appeared. My friend began to scream and tremble with fear, while I tried to reassure him, shouting that that animal was simply a cow and not a rhinoceros. My friend looked at me and said: "**Silly, I perfectly know that it is a cow, but I am afraid because a few days ago I burned myself with the milk.**" Unfortunately, this is how we react when we are afraid. The only way to overcome fear is to face everything that scares us with a calm mind, since it will increase our confidence in ourselves and allow us to face all of the obstacles and difficulties that we encounter throughout life.

There are different types of salespeople, for example, those selling in auto markets, those selling in stores, online, etc.

Most of them receive a salary plus a meager commission, because the entire sales process is generally carried out by the company or business. This is one of the reasons for the little interest that the salesperson shows towards customers. Furthermore, these companies have so many products that it is impossible for a salesperson to know them all. These are practically order pickers due to the little or no participation they have in the sales process. It is the same customers who buy the products and the salespeople only take the orders. It was not in vain when the great peasant leader Emiliano Zapata (1879-1919) known better as the "Caudillo del Sur", during the Mexican revolution, pronounced the following phrase: "**IF YOU WANT TO BE A BIRD, FLY. IF**

YOU WANT TO BE A WORM, CRAWL BUT DO NOT SCREAM WHEN THEY STEP ON YOU."

Unfortunately, many, many salespeople lack patience and want sales to go through immediately. All those who are dedicated to sales should know that this is impossible, because the conditions of the clients are extensive and varied, and therefore it is important to know how to qualify the prospect before meeting with them

The Salesperson or Professional Advisor who wishes to succeed must bear in mind that: **"Those who succeed are ordinary people with extraordinary determination."**

A good salesperson is an upright, healthy person, values friendship, is admired by their colleagues and friends, pays correctly and always fulfills what they promise. The bad salesperson is the complete opposite: a liar, a scammer, and their behavior sows many doubts. They will never have a future and are always surrounded by bad company. Which of the two would you like to be?

It is not necessary to be a liar. Sales is a privileged and unique profession. It takes talent, dedication and a lot of enthusiasm to become a true sales profesional. We just have to combine a few ingredients such as self-confidence, enthusiasm and a Positive Mental Attitude accompanied by a lot of hard work. This profession is not a friend of the lazy, careless and idler, it requires strong, honest, enthusiastic and disciplined people.

Negative people will never be able to prosper because of their fears, distrust in their abilities and the cowardice that paralyzes them and does not allow them to advance. They are people who want fast and

effective results, and of course, it does not work like that in our wonderful world of sales.

Consequently, I'd like to take a closer look at the different types of sales:

STORE SALES is the most common being the case of established businesses, where practically, as we said before, the entire sales process is carried out by the establishment or the company. They use good prices, offers, etc., all of this to attract hypothetical buyers, while all the salesperson does is, without much effort, place an order. In reality, in this type of sales, the buyer is the one who sells, since the effort of the salesperson is usually zero or almost zero. The

Russian novelist Fyodor Mikhailovich Dostoyevsky (1821-1881) is right when he says the following: "MAN IS A CREATURE THAT CAN GET ACCUSTOMED TO ANYTHING, AND I THINK THAT IS THE BEST DEFINITION OF HIM."

SALES IN AUTO-MARKETS: the buyer does not receive any kind of assistance since he himself picks up the products from the shelves and when he leaves, he pays. The Spanish political writer Vicente Blasco Ibáñez thought this way about these people who always complain about their bad economic situation

"The Poor Man Who Resigns Himself To His Luck And Does Not Seek To Get Rich, Be That As It May, By Hook Or By Crook, Is A Coward Or Useless, And Cannot Turn His Vileness Into A Merit."

ONLINE SALES: is the coldest and most impersonal that exists, since in most cases the salesperson and the buyer do not even know each other. The one who sells offers something through letters, catalogs or simply online, and whoever is interested in acquiring it requests it by mail, paying for it upon receipt, or in advance. This is how the Psychologist Bernardo Stamateas, an Argentine of Greek origin, refers to

comfort and conformism: **"COMFORT AND CONFORMISM ARE ENEMIES OF PASSION, GROWTH, DREAMS."**

SALES BY TELEPHONE: it is quite common but a prior personal contact with the client is almost always more necessary. It is a very practical way and it is also applied in direct sales.

MULTILEVEL MARKETING: Multilevel marketing is a form of direct sales where products are directly sold to the customers. Not only does the salesperson earn commissions on sales made by himself, but he also has residual income from the sales generated by the salesperson he associates with and teaches them to do the exact same thing. These recruits, in turn, can win other salespeople who will be part of the first level of the person who introduced them to the company and will be part of the second level of the original salesperson. In this way, the original salesperson, inspiring his salespeople, can gradually manufacture various levels, and can receive income on as many levels as each type of company allows.

The great thing about multi-level marketing is that you can have linear income through your sales and residual income on the levels that you will build from new salespeople learning to do the exact same thing.

These types of sales are sometimes very controversial. Many critics consider it fraudulent because they are very similar to pyramid schemes.

The candidate who wishes to enter this type of sales must, first of all, be well informed about the company's experience.

HYBRID SALES: Used by several companies, it refers to a mixed sales system between traditional direct or creative sales and multilevel. It is a very complicated system because the products to be sold are generally expensive and not consumable, that is, the customer buys only one time. Furthermore, the quota requirements to receive residual earnings from some companies are complex and difficult. This is the worst way to do business.

DIRECT OR CREATIVE SALES "Winning is not everything, but wanting to win is." Vince Lombardi

Direct sales are those where the entrepreneur and the salesperson

merge to commercialize goods and services, directly to prospects. The salesperson actually becomes the customer's personal Mentor, suggesting how he can best meet their needs. You must know how to apply the five basic principles of sales: **"AWAKEN CURIOSITY, AWAKEN INTEREST, AWAKEN DESIRE, AWAKEN THE NEED AND, OF COURSE, CLOSE THE SALE BY MAKING THE CONTRACT."**

Direct selling is, without a doubt, the most perfect and lucrative way for both the Advisor and the Client to do business, since there is direct contact between the Advisor and the prospect. For this reason, an unknown writer Florence Nightingale Stated: **"I ATTRIBUTE MY SUCCESS TO THIS: I NEVER GAVE OR TOOK AN EXCUSE."**

Every year more companies around the world join this way of marketing their products, and despite the fall of several economies such as Venezuela, Argentina and Uruguay, this growth in marketing products in direct sales also occurs throughout Latin America.

The reason for all this is that Direct Selling strengthens in times of crisis. Maybe it's because this system ships products directly to clients' homes and Consultants can show all the benefits without the client being distracted by the competitor's product.

Large Direct Selling corporations such as Avon Cosmetics, Rena Ware International, Herbalife, Mary Kay and many others that have been operating for many years with great success worldwide, have large numbers of successful Consultants who do not hesitate to face challenges and great difficulties -which exist especially in Latin America-, thanks to the excellent motivations of the Leaders and Companies.

Nowadays, it is not as easy as it seems to enter the sales world. To be successful in sales you need a series of factors, mainly in the outset. However, as a person gains experience and knowledge, he increases his confidence in himself and masters all the techniques of direct or creative sales.

In these times of economic instability, all men and women, with or without employment, seek the formula to earn more money because every day costs increase, making it difficult to maintain the standard of living they had.

Considering that most individuals do not have the time to work in two different places, the possibility of working in direct or creative sales makes it a fantastic activity as long as it is carried out with enthusiasm and keeping in mind that trust is the first great requirement to reach the achievements you need.

Surely, these suggestions related to selling can be of help to all who are interested in entering the oldest, **FANTABULOUS** and difficult profession: Sales. **"There is nothing more pleasant in life than doing what others thought would be imposible."** It also serves to improve your professionalism, and to those who are already involved in this fantastic and

fabulous profession, I wish for you to be powerful Leaders in your companies.

SECOND PART

ADVISOR PROFILE (SALESPERSON)

"Genius is one percent inspiration and ninety nine percent perspiration."

- Thomas Alva Edison.

Before we take a closer look at the direct selling business, let's reflect on this quote from Jim Cathcart, author, professional speaker and business leader, CEO of Cathcart Institute, Inc. (founded 1977), an organization dedicated to helping customers create and develop high-value relationships. **"BECOME THE PERSON WHO WOULD ATTRACT THE RESULTS YOU SEEK."**

Now we are ready to take a simple look at how most of these creative or direct selling businesses operate. Generally, in the most important cities they establish warehouses where the Consultants go and collect the products they sold.

Generally, direct sales companies will use offers or specials, to motivate and make the sale flow, and complicate the competition. Many times these strategies also serve to dispose of the excess of certain products in the warehouses.

A successful advisor needs to learn and put into practice a series of strategies that allow him to achieve the goal, as long as he applies the simple phrase of the 18th century American humorist Mark Twain when he stated: **"THE SECRET OF GETTING AHEAD IS GETTING STARTED."**

The salesperson's activity, as we said before, is one of the oldest activities in the world, but unfortunately it has never been valued for what it is really worth. One of the advantages of working in sales is that age does not matter, since the professional salesperson can, if they wish, make the sale at any age.

All companies should recognize the importance of the sales department in expanding markets. In addition, they must recognize that the salesperson is the best ally on the road to success.

In order to maintain a beneficial relationship between the company and the sales department, it is important that the company, in addition to having impeccable ethics with salespeople and customers, must continually invest in seminars and training materials to cultivate enthusiasm among its Advisors.

The art of sales is one of the most difficult and important activities, and the company must consider it as an asset on its balance sheet, because in reality the costs of the sales department are very low compared to other departments in the same company. Sales is considered an art and must be very well paid. The better the artist, the better your profit. As some unknown author said: **"EVERY DAY IS A NEW OPPORTUNITY TO CHANGE YOUR LIFE."**

The professional salesperson must be astute and intelligent to be able to answer quickly and honestly to the objections that the client raises during his sales visit. Regarding the latter, I remember a story I heard a long time ago about an old lion and a young fox. He spent every morning and afternoon in front of the cave where an old lion was and always greeted him: **"Good morning my king, how is your morning? I wish you have a good day."** The lion constantly invited him in, but the young fox always declined the invitation until one day the impatient old lion said to him **"But fox, when will you decide to visit me? Remember that I can't walk anymore."** The young fox replied, **"Never my king, never."** Surprised by the answer, the lion asked **"Why?"** The young fox replied: **"My King, I see**

footprints going in but I don't see footprints coming out." You must be a very astute person like the young fox because you must learn to respond quickly, with logic and conviction to all the objections that the prospect raises.

As the third president of the United States of America Thomas Jefferson (1743-1826) stated, to know what you are worth, **"DO YOU WANT TO KNOW WHO YOU ARE? DO NOT ASK. ACT! ACTION WILL DELINEATE AND DEFINE YOU."**

Being a professional Advisor is not an easy task,but it is not an impossible, with experience and dedication and a lot of faith you will gain confidence, which will help you increase your enthusiasm and acquire the necessary Positive Mental Attitude, transforming you into a successful

Sales Professional. Someone said: **"A Smooth Sea Never Made A Skilled Sailor."**

Here are a series of suggestions for you to begin to reinvent yourself and successfully overcome the challenges that life's circumstances present daily.

1. You must be detail oriented, to be able to carry out all your plans.

2. You must be highly competitive, this is a powerful motivation that leads you to make extra efforts to achieve a goal.

3. You must have curiosity as a quality to help you learn easily and satisfy with your work.

4. You must have great tolerance, mainly in leadership positions where you make decisions for the common good.

5. You must have a great capacity for change to be able to face all difficulties and work under pressure.

Here are some positive quotes from some unknown authors that have motivated many sales champions, because to achieve goals you need some extra stimuli, and believe me, these come only from yourself.

1. **"THE BEST TIME TO PLANT A TREE WAS 20 YEARS AGO. THE SECOND BEST MOMENT IS NOW."**

2. "POSITIVE PEOPLE ARE THOSE WHO FALL, GET UP, SHAKE, HEAL THEIR SCRATCHES, SMILE AT LIFE AND SAY, DESTINY IS NOT BASED ON LUCK BUT ON DETERMINATION."

Get inspired, don't be afraid. Rather, have a lot of confidence and a Positive Mental Attitude and you will inevitably be a winner.

You must be convinced that you do not sell anything, on the contrary, you are an Advisor, and under your direction and advice it is the client who buys. In other words, with your advice you satisfy the wishes and needs of the client, who automatically acquires the product or service that you provide.

As an Advisor you should keep the following in mind:

- **Understand what the customer wants.**

- Always maintain a successful attitude. People like to do business with successful people and not with losers.
- Be nice.
- Be prepared to make a very, very good presentation of the product or service that you represent, showing the added value.
- Anticipate objections and propose the solution to fill the needs.
- Quickly understand the objections and needs of customers, always having a convincing response.
- Never push, but be firm at the time of closing the sale, so that the customer feels comfortable.
- Don't promise things you can't keep, always keep your promises.
- Good communication.
- Your Positive Mental Attitude is essential not only in sales but also throughout your life.

- The worst thing you can do is lie to do business.

I remember when I joined Rena Ware International 52 years ago. At the end of the training they gave us a little steel plate that said: **"OUR MOTTO IS HONESTY."** And throughout my years this was always the course that I followed.

As a good Advisor you must:

- Show the customer how your product or service can HELP.
- Remember the Universal law that to receive we must give, never forget it.
- It is very important when conducting a business that you always think about whether your client was satisfied and do not focus on your profit.

- When you work well and honestly, money comes by itself. Remember, a satisfied customer is future profit.

- What matters most in life is having a great goal and possessing the ability and perseverance to achieve it.

The characteristics of sales professionals:

Good Presence: You can tell a professional as soon as they walk through the door because they care about the way they dress, their overall appearance and they radiate confidence and security.

Honor: All professionals feel honored by their profession and by themselves. They feel worthy of the services they provide.

Confidence: Self-confidence is mainly acquired when we learn to do the things that scare us the most, such as cold door knocking, speaking in public, not giving in to the first negative response from the client, etc. Only by practicing will you grow the confidence you need to be successful.

Cordiality: With cordiality, sales professionals know how to advise their prospect by closing the sale. Their techniques are firm, but they know how to present them with cordiality and sympathy, almost always obtaining the desired results.

Self-confidence: All professionals develop a lot of confidence thanks to the great confidence they have in themselves.

They are successful: Professionals constantly prepare by improving all of their techniques, so that when they are in front of a prospect they can achieve the sale.

Professionals dare to do what they fear: they know what their fears are, they attack them, and they surpass them, in this way their confidence constantly grows in them.

They overcome all problems with enthusiasm : they always maintain their enthusiasm. They feel optimistic about life, they are happy, that is why they have a super excellent Positive Mental Attitude.

All professionals constantly invest to increase knowledge and study new techniques. They are always looking to generate positive changes and acquire more knowledge to improve all the things that gravitate around them.

The Sales Professional analyzes very well who their prospect is. They will take the time to know about:

- What your economic level is?
- How your family is?

- What your tastes are?
- Where does our client live?
- How old you are?

In addition, the following recommendations should be beard in mind:

- Listen to your customer.
- Anticipate their objections.
- Always try to satisfy their needs.
- Keep in touch with your customer.
- Observe how theirb habits, customs, tastes, and needs change.
- Be quick and honest in your answers.
- Add value to your products.
- Excellently connect with your customers.
- Win the trust of your customers.
- Be credible.

- Advise your clients in making the most convenient decision for them, when acquiring your product or service.

As an advisor, you must also be:

- Different from the majority of the other Advisors.
- Maintain an impeccable personality.
- You must be unique, original and creative.
- Be a pioneer in everything you do, use your own personality.
- Make a big difference with the competitors.

Finally, we must do what the great self-help book writer Og Mandino used to say: "**Exercise your privilege to go the extra mile.**" Let's try to better analyze its profund meaning. Mainly, walking one more mile means to effectively finish the things we started. It means not giving up before finishing, not being aware of the time your day ends because it ends when your task is finished. This extra mile is the one that successful Leaders travel because they know that merit sows trust, trust sows enthusiasm, enthusiasm increases our Positive Mental Attitude and this conquers the world, allowing you to rise in leadership positions in the Sales companies. This is what great leaders do to achieve success. **I invite you to walk the extra mile.**

It is not by chance that one of the richest and most successful businessman, Aristotle Onasis started out as a salesman. He claimed: **"WE HAVE TO LEARN TO SAIL IN HIGH WINDS."**

Characteristics of the successful Advisor (Salesperson):

1.- **Unlimited success**: Successful salespeople constantly want to overcome their past successes. They are increasingly exceeding themselves. They are like athletes, they always want to break their own record

2.- **They are not afraid**: Did you know that fear defeats more people than anything else in life? Thanks to their excellent confidence, they maintain a Positive Mental attitude, helping them overcome all their fears. The best Advisors fear nothing, they blindly trust their abilities and the company.

3.- **Positive Mental Attitude**: Your confidence accompanied by a very excellent Positive Mental Attitude helps you conquer and overcome all fears. They know that there are always many positive opportunities waiting, you just have to find them.

4.- **Realism**: Successful salespeople are realistic, they have their feet on the ground and they know when to close a sale with a customer. They don't believe in false expectations, they quickly detect when time is being wasted and when it pays to be persistent.

5.- **Product knowledge**: Professional salespeople are not limited to the basic knowledge learned in training, they continually investigate the characteristics of their products or services.

6.- **Passion for the profession**: They feel proud to belong to the oldest profession in the world and to help many prospects to improve their living conditions.

The true professional knows that the harder he works, the greater his fortune.

The personality of the advisor:

The personality of a professional Advisor (Salesperson) must have two fundamental characteristics that influence their success: the first is **honesty**, the second **mental ability**.

If you want professional success, first sell your personality before your products, such as:

- Character

- Energy

- Perseverance

- Enthusiasm

- Sincerity

- Self control

- Self-confidence

- Sympathy

- Sense of humor

- Mental ability

- Intelligence

- Attention

- Memory

- Clarity and precision of ideas

- Weighting

- Communicability and empathy

  - Be honest with yourself, frankly analyze yourself and try to know how others see you.

  - Find out if you have habits or actions that generally annoy others.

- If you smile it is almost certain that you will be able to break the possible barriers that exist to achieve success.

- Do not breathe on the other person when you are speaking. Don't get too close to him, don't run him over.

- Demonstrate that you are not only capable of hearing, but that you are also capable of listening. Do not speak too loud nor too low, beware of a squeaky voice, do not speak too fast or too slow. The best way for our interlocutor to comfortably follow what you are trying to explain is by involving them with frequently asked questions.

- Take care of your personal hygiene, the cleanliness of your hands and nails, use a not very strong perfume. Many Salespeople miss out on great opportunities because of this oversight.

- Do not smoke or drink, apart from being harmful to your health, most clients do not like to deal with people whose breath smells of smoke or alcohol. If you want to, do it when you decide not to work.

- Eliminate all nervous tics. For example, avoid rocking in the seat, do not direct your gaze to the ceiling or behind the client, look straight ahead.

I want to end this second part with another excellent phrase from Aristotle Socrates Onassis, who as a salesman became one of the most

important businessmen of the 20th century: **"I MIGHT AGE QUICKLY, BUT I WILL STRUGGLE SO THAT IT WOULD HAVE BEEN WORTH MY DAY."**

THIRD PART

SALES PROCESS

"We must learn to sail in high winds."

Aristotle Socrates Onasis

As I said before, we are all salespeople and all, unconsciously or consciously, use the five great principles of sales:

Arouse curiosity,

Awaken the interest,

Awaken the desire,

Awaken the need

And close the sale.

These are the mandatory steps for all of us in sales. If we want to be good professionals, we must master the sales process very well.

Taking into account that the sales profession is considered among the most difficult, it is also one of the best paid. In fact, after good artists, who are the best paid in the world, good Salespeople are considered first cousins of artists because they must act and have the ability to win the attention and trust of customers.

If you are or plan to be a salesperson, you should keep the following tips in mind to achieve excellence:

1.- Understand that sales is one of the most difficult and complicated professions out there, but it is very well paid.

2.- Have a specific goal that motivates you, the goal should be annual, monthly, weekly and daily.

3.- Make a daily work plan to achieve the goal and do not abandon it until you have reached the pre-established daily goal.

4.- Know that, as a salesperson, the only time you produce money is when you are face to face with a potential buyer.

5.- Know that the greater the number of prospects visited, demonstrating the benefits of your product or service, the greater the number of closed contracts.

6.- Know that for a salesperson the art of getting an appointment with potential clients is extremely important for the development of their profession.

7.- Know the averages of appointments and sales of your specialty very well and work with them.

8.- Remember that the results are directly proportional to the number of prospects visited.

9.- Success in sales does not depend on the economic circumstances of a country. If your country is in an unfavorable situation, you will need to increase the number of visits.

Most of the suggestions I have given you are those that most professional salespeople have employed. I know from experience that they work well.

You cannot become an excellent professional salesperson overnight, you must start small with a lot of patience, faith, intelligence, confidence, enthusiasm and a Positive Mental Attitude. It is then that you will become an excellent professional salesperson and in this way you will conquer the world.

Remember what the Chinese say: **"A LONG JOURNEY ALWAYS STARTS WITH THE FIRST STEP"**. Take the first step to being the great person hidden within you.

The sales process is the succession of steps that a sales professional takes from the moment they gain the attention of a potential prospect to its conclusion. That is, until an effective sale of the product or service that is represented is achieved.

The sales process goes through several points:

CURIOSITY: In this phase the Advisor tries to draw the attention of his potential clients to his product or service. You can do this using many techniques, but all of them must be related to the final action that will be the sale.

INTEREST: Once we have captured the customer's attention, we must awaken their interest. How can a professional salesperson achieve it? Using his sympathy and mainly a lively chat that forces the client to be attentive in everything that is said.

DESIRE: If the Advisor captured curiosity and interest, it is very likely that the prospect will come to feel a desire to own the product. The Advisor will awaken the desire by means of a very excellent presentation of their products or services, also asking questions that the client answers with a conditional YES, for example: "will you agree with me that with the use of this or that product / service you will save time and money? Absolutely right! 99.99% of the times the client will answer affirmatively. You are automatically transmitting positive information to their brain that leads them to desire the product or service that you distribute. This should be done throughout your presentation. Thus, the client gradually goes from desire to need to possess what is offered.

NEED: through the demonstration of the sales professional that awakens the desire in the client - with specific questions and teaching that the value of the product or service is very flattering with respect to the benefits-, it is then when the client feels they need it, a nd he's ready to hear your offer. The professional salesperson immediately begins the last phase of the process.

CLOSURE OF SALES: If the client goes through all these phases, they will reach the final phase, which is the closing of the sale. In this phase the prospect is already convinced of what he wants and, therefore, the economic transaction and the purchase of the good or service takes place.

Closing sales is a positive relationship between two people. In this phase, each prospect should be treated as if they were the most important person in the world. In addition, when you make a quality sales closing, it will satisfy both you and your prospect, who will become your friend. This relationship will endure over time as long as you are the same honest person that the customer saw when the deal was closed. Our customers-friends will always be loyal to us, and when you use the 'win-win'

principle with them, satisfied customers will not only return, they will bring in more customers. **BE A TRUE MENTOR TO YOUR CLIENTS.**

FOURTH PART

THE ART OF SELLING

"Motivation is almost always

meer talent."

Norman Ralph Augustine.

Usually, a lot of people are totally wrong about selling. If we analyze the origin and true meaning of "to sell", this word comes from the Latin *venum dare* which means "'to give to sell". Unfortunately, as the selling profession expanded this meaning morphed into "cheat the prospect". Fortunately, nowadays the large sales companies define it as **"to persuade"**.

When a person wishes to enter sales, they will understand that their function is to Advise, honestly persuading the prospect to acquire a product or service that benefits them. It can be said that the sale is a "conversation" with the purpose of advising, persuading the prospect-client to decide to make the purchase of the product or service, which will fill both the customer and the salesperson with satisfaction.

In fact, in order to achieve success as a salesperson you must like sales. Sales do not depend on your "crude talk", but on honest advice to the client, in order to cultivate a lasting relationship between the two.

Since you cannot force a prospect-customer to buy, you must use the sales process by exposing the benefits of the products or services that the prospect-customer will receive in order for them to decide to buy.

After you've made the sale, it's good to stay in touch with your customer by worrying about how the product or service works. By doing so, you

will earn their trust and the customer will recomend you to their friends, associates, and acquaintances, who will potentially become new customers.

For this reason, we affirm that to dedicate yourself to sales you do not need to learn magic tricks. Simply apply the sales process with honesty: Awaken Curiosity, Awaken Interest, Awaken Desire, Awaken Need. If all this is well done, the Closing of the sale will turn out automatically.

It is important to know the candidate-client, as well as knowing the product or service you offer, and how this is going to solve the needs of the prospect.

The success in the sale of your product or service depends on your ability to advise and honestly persuade the client. In this way you guarantee that the prospect acquires the product or service from you and not from another person.

Keeping in mind that the first thing a client buys is trust, you must be able to honestly advise them in order to achieve this in the prospect, thus making the decision to make the purchase. If they don't trust you and don't feel confident in what you say, they won't buy anything from you and they'll find what they're looking for elsewhere.

Most salespeople work on their prospects superficially. They don't understand that people always **buy out of emotion**. For this reason, our arguments must - in addition to being convincing - excite the prospect by making them dream of the great benefits they would enjoy acquiring the product or service that you presented them. Clients want to be sure that they are making the right decision and there the importance of their advice. To make them feel confident, they need conviction that only you can convey through genuine enthusiasm.

Curiosity is one of the virtues of professional salespeople. They want to know more about their clients, their needs, personal desires, fears, and concerns.

Sales professionals do not try to bombard the customer with idle talk. They are specialists in asking specific questions to try to find out what their true needs, wishes, concerns or fears are in relation to the product and service they are presenting.

Remember what the CEO of Cycnus Marketing, one of the largest professional networks in the world, Leonardo Benijes said: **"THE MORE YOU KNOW, THE MORE YOU SELL. IT IS NOT THE MORE I TALK, THE MORE I SELL."**

The Sales Professional with their genuine enthusiasm attract the prospect to their arguments, thus establishing a positive communication between

Advisor and client, which almost always ends with a contract.

The Professional continually reinforces credibility in everything that is enthusiastically exposed, increasing the possibility of sale. The enthusiasm of the Advisor produces an empathy with the client who decides to purchase the product or service it represents.

We must fight to eradicate from our thoughts ideas such as: "our prices are very high", "our products are not complete","my city is out of stock", "in December they stop buying", "they do not open the door", "it is difficult in these times to get appointments", etc ... With statements like these the salesperson pretends to excuse themselves, their colleagues and leaders, for their lack of success. Unfortunately, these are mainly the causes of their failure.

Errors that the professional advisor must avoid:

1.- **Talking too quickly**. It is a typical insecure beginner's mistake to try to reach the end. Try to speak, instead, as if your ideas are evolving as you go through your presentation.

2.- **Take care of your language**. The excessive use of idioms and marginal idioms should be avoided.

3.- **Monotonous.** Frequently, in Standard demonstrations, which even the salesperson finds boring, one falls into the linear and does not give voice or expressions or enriches the exposition with appropriate examples.

4.- **Not be numbing**. Never allow your exposure to wane. Practice eliminates inaccuracies. Don't get cornered. Keep final questions, several aces up your sleeve.

5.- Inability to summarize. The inability to summarize sometimes makes the conversation that started well, tend to "sink" as it progresses.

6.- Bored. Use your first words to bring up the points of interest, they will keep the customer awake and encourage them to participate.

7.- Never spend too much time. That happens when the exhibitor deviates, pretending to improvise without having enough practice.

"THE MOST IMPORTANT PERSUASION TOOL YOU HAVE IN YOUR ENTIRE ARSENAL IS INTEGRITY." **Zig Ziglar**

FIFTH PART

PROFESSIONAL ETHICS

"Ethics is knowing the difference between what you have a right to do and what is right to do."

Potter Stewart

"IN WORKING FOR SYMPATHY, FOR COMPASSION, FOR CHARITY, THERE IS ABSOLUTELY NO MORALITY." **IMMANUAL KANT** The word "ethics" derives from the Greek ethos which means "way of doing things". It also refers to the branch of philosophy that studies behavior. Simón Bolívar knew human weaknesses very well, for this reason he once declared **"MORALS AND LIGHTS ARE OUR PRIMARY NEEDS."**

By ethics we refer to a series of rules and regulations that regulate human relationships, including all professions. This is how the historian and political scientist James MacGregor Burns (1918-2014) describes ethics, **"DIVORCED FROM ETHICS, LEADERSHIP IS REDUCED TO MANAGEMENT AND POLITICS TO MERE TECHNIQUE."**

Professional ethics in sales is defined by the Advisor's behavior in the development of his profession. **As we said before**, professional ethics consists of a set of values that regulate the way in which the

Professional Advisor should behave with their prospects and with the company.

Sales ethics is the honest behavior that the advisor must maintain with the prospect, putting aside personal interests and protecting the interests of the prospect. For this reason, the great Roman philosopher, politician and orator Marcus Tullius Cicero (106 BC-43 BC) referred to ethics, **"MY CONSCIENCE HAS MORE WEIGHT FOR ME THAN THE OPINION OF THE WHOLE WORLD."**

It is very important not to confuse morality with ethics: morality is when a person respects the rules, even if they do not agree with those that exist in the society in which they live. Ethics is as defined by jazz trumpeter Wynton Marsalis (1961), **"ETHICS ARE MORE IMPORTANT THAN LAWS."**

There are some universal values that we must all respect such as: **"FREEDOM, RESPECT, HONESTY, UNDERSTANDING, JUSTICE AND FRIENDSHIP."** These should guide our path of life.

Not in vain the famous novelist, playwright and essayist Albert Camus (1913-1960) stated in one of his lectures, **"A MAN WITHOUT ETHICS IS A WILD BEAST LOOSED UPON THIS WORLD."**

The universal values of ethics are very important and are today, more or less accepted by all of the organizations to try to regulate relationships between individuals, making life develop without manipulations and are instead, full of pleasant opportunities for everyone.

Ethics and success are always together. The successful Advisor always has great ethics. The following are important points to strengthen ethics and success:

1.- Consider all of the secrets that are entrusted to you as a personal secret.

2.- Everything you say must be true. But you are not always obliged to tell everything, not even the whole truth.

3.- Take care of what third parties can deduce from your words.

4.- The small client deserves the same treatment as the large client.

5.- Do not try to be important by disseminating confidential company information. A secret to three ceases to be.

.6.- You should never spread suspicions regarding the private life of another person.

7.- Play deaf to anyone who wants to communicate highly confidential information.

"ETHICS IS NOTHING OTHER THAN REVERENCE FOR LIFE." Albert Schweitzer

SIXTH PART

THE POWER OF TRUST

"The way to develop self-confidence
is to do what you fear and keep track of
your successful experiences."

William Jennings Bryan

Trust is important for the relationship between human beings and helps the person who possesses it for their personal growth. We must bear in mind that all relationships are based on trust.

If trust was lacking, there would be no relationship, from the couple to the relationships with companies. **"SELF-TRUST IS THE FIRST SECRET OF SUCCESS".** This is how Ralp Waldo Emerson (1803-1882), American poet and philosopher, defined trust.

Napoleon Bonaparte, (1769-1821) one of the greatest military generals and strategists, as well as the first emperor of France, is considered one of the most important military leaders in the world. Napoleon revolutionized military organization and training, sponsored the Napoleonic Code, reorganized education, and established the lasting concordat with the papacy. This is how he pronounced himself with regard to trust, **"WE ARE MADE WEAK BOTH BY IDLENESS AND DISTRUST OF OURSELVES."**

Having trust gives us a sense of security that makes us feel comfortable with respect to another person. It is, without a doubt, the most important thing so that the professional Advisor can close the sale. For this reason, Professional Advisors who develop great self-trust are the ones who achieve success most quickly. It is important that our prospects trust us, only in this way can we establish good and lasting relationships.

Trust begins with oneself, with our principles, knowledge, and thus we will advance safely and with confidence in our life. Having confidence should not transform you into a presumptuous or haughty person, it should be the opposite: a simple, kind, sincere and honest person. These qualities will allow you to face the challenges that life presents.

Perhaps you have never considered it, but the best thing you can do to become a great sales professional is to be a trustworthy person. Zig Ziglar (1926-2012), American writer, salesperson, and motivational speaker referred to trust this way, **"IF PEOPLE LIKE YOU, THEY WILL LISTEN TO YOU, BUT IF THEY TRUST YOU, THEY WILL DO BUSINESS WITH YOU."**

Trust is the security that an Advisor demonstrates in their performance. It is important for the sales professional to have this power. Here are some important points in order to develop it.

1.-: The only way to have confidence in yourself is through practice. This comes from experience, which is only obtain thanks to your willingness to face obstacles and difficult situations.

2.-: The true secret of a successful Salesperson is the absolute confidence one has in oneself and in one's abilities.

3.-: The Advisor who has confidence in himself or herself helps them face their defects with all honesty, and consequently forces him or her to make corrections.

4.-: The confidence that a professional Advisor has in themselves allows one to clearly set their goals and create a desire with enough force to overcome all obstacles.

5.-: Action is the test of true self-confidence. The self-confident Advisor can motivate others because he or she is self-motivated. Self-confidence is the key to all achievement because it reinforces skill, doubles energy, expands mental capacity, and increases personal strength.

In this regard, Socrates, the philosopher, (470-399 BC) considered the forerunner of philosophy and thought in the West **said "DO NOT LET GRASS GROW ON THE PATH OF FRIENDSHIP."**

SEVENTH PART

THE POWER OF MOTIVATION

"Motivation is what gets you started.
Habit is what keeps you going."

- Jim Ryun

K'ung Fu-tzu, better known as Confucius (551-479 BC), was a Chinese thinker from a noble family. Throughout his life he alternated periods in which he served as a teacher and in others in which he served as an official of the small state of Lu, in northeast China during the time of fragmentation of power under the Chu dynasty. Confucius defined life regarding motivation as follows, **"IT DOESN'T MATTER HOW SLOWLY YOU GO AS LONG AS YOU DO NOT STOP."**

Motivation can be defined as the interest that a Salesperson has towards a certain need, in this way creating and increasing the necessary impulse to achieve certain things.

Motivation is the union of the words Motive + Action. Therefore, when an Advisor has an important goal, they will take action to achieve it. In short, the power of motivation is an impulse that makes us act, and leads us towards a goal.

We are all motivated - some more than others - but the leader, specially, must have the ability to persevere in the goal, move mountains and execute their vision. The motivation also indicates the contribution that the Salesperson is willing to give to the company. The radio host and author of human development issues Earl Nightingale (1921-1989) stated in one of his voice-overs, **"WE HAVE BECOME THE FRUIT OF OUR THOUGHTS."**

Motivated Advisors are oriented toward the pursuit of success. Money is not the most important thing, although they aspire to acquire wealth in their effort to reach the goal, what counts is the goal and with it, the triumph. They are motivated to overcome obstacles because they know that overcoming them will mean reaching their goal.

The truth is that in companies where there are many Salespeople able to motivate themselves to improve their quality of life, these have a much faster development than others.

According to the above, we could say that the need for self-realization is really a necessity for all those who want to become professional Advisors, achieving success in their company. In this sense, motivation is an impulse that allows you to control situations. Advisors motivated to achieve their goals tend to accept risk more easily. Napoleon Hill (1883-1970) is considered the most influential man in history to lead people to success. Here is one of his most famous phrase, **"ANYTHING THAT THE MIND OF MAN CAN CONCEIVE AND BELIEVE, CAN BE ACHIEVED."**

Some ideas to unleash the power of motivation in you:

1.- Self-motivation is the force that elevates an Advisor to whatever level they wish to reach.

2.- Those Advisors who really want to be successful have the responsibility to motivate themselves and can start on their own, because they have their own spark within.

3.- A common cause of human failure is total disregard to the force of self-motivation.

4.- It is impossible to motivate another person before having learned to motivate yourself.

5.- There are always opportunities for Consultants who understand and apply self-motivation.

6.- A self-motivated Advisor makes commitments, common Advisors make promises.

7.- What we achieve in life depends on the importance of our goal, which will give us the reason to act.

8.- The strength of motivation comes from the goal and a defined action plan.

9.- The Advisor who never discovers his own motivation is equivalent to being a mental invalid.

EIGHTH PART

POWER OF GOALS

"If you want to reach a goal, you must see the reaching in your own mind before you actually arrive at your goal."- Zig Ziglar

James Cash "JC" Penney Jr. (1875-1971) was a businessman and entrepreneur who founded the famous JC Penney department store chain in 1902. These were his ideas regarding goals, **"GIVE ME AN ORDINARY EMPLOYEE BUT WITH A GOAL AND I WILL GIVE YOU A MAN WHO MAKES HISTORY. GIVE ME AN EXCEPTIONAL MAN WHO HAS NO GOALS AND I'LL GIVE YOU AN ORDINARY MAN."**

We all have dreams on our mind. Usually they are poorly defined dreams, without a specific plan, such as becoming a millionaire, living in a wonderful house or going around the world. However, very few are those who have clear goals with a well-defined plan and are willing to fight hard to achieve them.

We should honestly ask ourselves, what do we really want to achieve in our life?

-If we have a true desire to achieve a goal then we are ready to start fighting hard and of course, we will also be willing to overcome all obstacles.

-With trust and faith we will develop the necessary enthusiasm to have a Positive Mental Attitude that will be the energy that moves all of our actions. If we do not have a Positive Mental Attitude, all our goals are unattainable.

-Your goal must be real and credible and not a fantastic illusion.

- A great goal is not achieved overnight, which is why we must have a lot of patience and tenacity. It is convenient to set goals for short and medium terms so that we can gradually get closer to the final goal.

- For any goal to make sense, we must develop an action plan and then carry it out. Be careful with excuses, as it is easy to justify yourself for giving up on reaching the goal. Unfortunately, we the Salespeople are adept at making excuses to deviate from our purpose. When excuses prevent us from reaching our goal, it means that the goal we had was not really what we wanted. This is why it is important that when we set a goal for ourselves we must intensely desire it. For this reason someone used to say, **"EVERYTHING THAT I VIVELY IMAGINE, I ARDENTLY DESIRE, SINCERELY CREATE AND ENTHUSIASTICALLY ACHIEVE WILL INEVITABLY BE DONE."**

Beware of your fears, as they appear when you look away from your goal and can destroy all your desires. Fear is the reaction that occurs before a real or imaginary danger. In Sales, the Advisor is afraid of failure, of being wrong, or of being criticized by others. Whatever the fear may be, it represents the greatest obstacle that the Advisor must overcome in order to achieve their goals and with it success.

There are no magical formulas. Only we can find the strength to fight for our goals. You must work intelligently, with perseverance and a lot of Positive Mental Attitude. If you don't try hard enough to achieve your goal, you will never know if you could have achieved it. Lucius Annaeus Seneca, the most representative philosopher of Stoicism (4th century BC) and one of the most important figures in philosphy during the Roman Republic, once stated the following: **"IF ONE DOES NOT KNOW TO WHICH PORT ONE IS SAILING, NO WIND IS FAVORABLE."**

By virtue of the Advisor being able to develop a profitable activity, it is necessary to daily maintain clear and real goals, in this way we will have the necessary motivation to achieve them.

The goal is the end to which you direct your actions. We all have short, medium and long term goals in life. These are the objectives where we must direct all of our efforts and motivation.

1.- If a person is not making the progress they want, they should simply review their goals, which may not be very clear, and redesign the action plan.

2.- When a salesperson sets his own goals, they work in two ways: the the Salesperson works to achieve them and they act on the motivation of the Salesperson.

3.- Goal setting should never be confused with wishes or illusions. The Advisor who sets a realistic goal is taking the first step toward positive performance of his or her duties.

4.- Goal setting is the most powerful human force for success in life.

5.- The world is full of people who have stayed where they are simply because their goals do not take them anywhere.

6.- The goals that a person sets for themselves constitute the prelude to action, the way to go, the route to be followed.

7.- Nobody can achieve anything of importance unless they set a goal.

8.- Once a goal has been set, one must firmly and unambiguously believe that it will be achieved, and the greater the confidence, the faster the progress.

9.- Each of us is born to construct our own destiny. The depth of what we reach is measured by the goals we set for ourselves.

NINTH PART

THE POWER OF ENTHUSIASM

"Years may wrinkle the skin,
but to give up interest wrinkles
the soul."

Albert Schweitzer

Enthusiasm is **a state of mind that is considered an "effervescence"** before a fact or situation in life. When we speak of enthusiasm, we are hinting about an emotion that takes over our general state for one or more minutes. Enthusiasm is the ability to manage emotions. For the Greeks, enthusiasm meant "having a god within oneself." The enthusiastic person, therefore, was one guided by the strength and wisdom of a God, capable of making fantabulous things happen.

Enthusiasm is considered **one of the most positive states of mind** that a person can feel, since they are those moments in which everything seems to have a certain meaning and desire for something to happen. Many times enthusiasm is spoken of as a quality that a person can acquire, however, it is only an emotional state **that can arise at any time** and in any person in a certain situation. Not everyone feels the same interest and motivation for the same goals.

It is said that enthusiasm is not produced by doing things well, but rather the opposite. Enthusiasm is what makes us do things well. It is necessary for a person to have confidence and faith, which will give them the necessary enthusiasm to be able to carry out everything they propose. It is the ability to transform everything that surrounds us and turn it into something positive for oneself.

What is truly real is that many professional Salespeople who succeed and maintain a leadership position in the company are because they have a lot of enthusiasm. Let's analyze what enthusiasm is and what it means to you. That is why it is important to talk about the power of enthusiasm.

Here are some procedures for developing and maintaining the power of enthusiasm:

1.- Enthusiasm is the way a Salesperson squeezes the trigger of emotions.

2.- Enthusiasm is the primary method of persuasion without pressure.

3.- The enthusiastic Advisor shines, radiates, penetrates and immediately captures everyone's interest.

4.- Enthusiasm predisposes and prepares the professional salesperson for new ideas.

5.- Enthusiasm does not make people educated, but it does makes them write history.

6.- Enthusiasm is the greatest wealth. If a person is taken from their money and all tangible property, but allowed to retain his or her enthusiasm, in a very short time he or she will be as rich as before.

7.- Enthusiasm is the product of trust and faith that makes us exclaim before the whole world, "I have what I need."

8.- Enthusiasm allows the Salesperson to compete with themselves, to look at the results of the past to overcome them in the present. Only with the impulse of enthusiasm can you overcome past mistakes.

9.- Enthusiasm is that wonderful state of mind that elevates Salespeople to the highest levels.

The problem of maintaining enthusiasm is sometimes very complicated and difficult because enthusiasm generally tends to wane due to disappointments, frustrated hopes, etc. All of this tends to diminish enthusiasm, but in reality this will happen if the Salesperson allows it. Enthusiasm

makes a huge difference over the ultimate results in your life. As Huxley said, **"The secret of genius is to carry the spirit of the child into old age, which means never losing your enthusiasm."**

TENTH PART

THE POWER OF SUCCESS

"A successful man is one who is capable of doing what others are too lazy to do."

Ignacio Orrego Rojo

"THERE ARE NO ELEVATORS TO SUCCESS, YOU HAVE TO TAKE THE STAIRS." - Zig Ziglar Success, in general, is associated with accomplishment in something that we set out to do, as well as obtaining recognition due to our merits.

As Ben Sweetland said, keep in mind that: **"SUCCESS IS A JOURNEY, NOT A DESTINATION."** Every time you reach a goal, you must immediately have another one and strive hard to achieve it. You must do so throughout your life to enjoy it and feel proud of having lived a successful life.

Do not be afraid and do not limit your thoughts. You must think big and give big to be able to receive big. You must learn to make decisions, no one can make them for you. Your decisions are exclusively yours, they are part of you, like the air you breathe every day of your life. Be a determined person, act now, but well. Dare to be a winner.

Booker T. Washington used to say, "**SUCCESS ISTO BE MEASURED NOT SO MUCH BY THE POSITION THAT ONE HAS REACHED IN LIFE AS BY THE OBSTACLES WHICH HE HAS OVERCOME.**"

Being a successful Salesperson is relatively easy, we just have to be a woman or man with a lot of enthusiasm. Remember that we are the result of all of our thoughts. It is precisely our thoughts that help us create our future. If you only change your thoughts, you will change the course of your life.

We all have the power to achieve success, the only thing we must do is awaken our enthusiasm and use the Positive Mental Attitude to achieve the goals that we have set. We must always and only think positive. You will be amazed at the wonderful things that will happen to you. If, on the other hand, you think negative things you will only get failures.

With a strong Positive Mental Attitude we will attract only wonderful things and we will be happy winners.

When asked how he managed to win such a difficult race, the 8-year-old world champion of the International Bicicross Federation, Luis Roberto García replied: **"All I did was pedal and pedal. I felt great and knew that I would win. That's why I didn't look anywhere or worry about those who were coming after me. I knew the best way to win was to fully concentrate on the test."** The world belongs to the people who are willing to give 200% of what is expected of them.

Remember that if you never work more than what you are paid, you will never get more for what you work.

Success in life depends on your ability to make everyone you interact with daily feel good. There are many writings on how to achieve success in life, but there are few who read it and very few who practice it.

I want to share a few easy tips that anyone with two fingers on their forehead and a little will can practice. **"you must live each day of your life with optimism and you will see how happy you will feel."** Remember that you are what you think and what you want to be. This is why it is important to think positive things and wish the best for yourself, wishing to achieve success every day will get you in to the habit of achieving success.

You must develop a strong confidence in yourself and in your abilities. Also, focus on reaching your goal with determination, without losing confidence due to obstacles, criticism and difficulties. One idea is enough so you can achieve fame and fortune. Always use kind words, they will increase the number of your friends. Finally, keep in mind that you attract what you think, so it is important to feel respect for yourself and others. Lastly, have clear and definitive ideas to achieve your goals.

You must cancel all those negative thoughts from your mind: **rejection, criticism, failure, ridicule, fear of the unknown, doing new things, ridicule, fear of paying a price.**

Overcome the fears that paralyze you and keep you from success with the following measures: **"have clear and precise goals, have a plan to achieve them, seek the opportunity, train every day, always act with respect, do not abandon halfway." In short, WORK, WORK AND WORK HARD.** Remember that the body gets sick if your mind gives it permission.

Here are some tips on the power of success:

1.- Few people can be truly successful just by chance or by a stroke of luck. Effective success depends on the degree to which your potential is used and developed.

2.- Success has always been and will always be the natural result of what a person is and not what he pretends to be.

3.- A person must evaluate and weigh their own talent and the abilities that constitute their potential.

4.- The simplest definition of Success is: the progressive realization of a predetermined goal.

5.- Does a successful person achieve the impossible? NO! He limits himself to doing what most of the critics thought impossible to do.

6.- The successful person makes as many mistakes as any other person. The crucial difference lies in learning something from each of these mistakes.

7.- The only honest measure of success that a person achieves is what they are doing compared to their true potential.

8. Make the decision that you will succeed, then invest every grain of your mental and physical energy in the effort to make it happen.

9.- Anyone can be successful for a single day if they want to. You have to fight mightily, learn as much as possible, cultivate understanding and try to achieve each goal, then do the same the next day and so on.

10.- Success is just another way of naming the unlimited capacity that a person has to become more creative, understanding, courageous, humble, useful and dynamic.

John Ruskin (1819-1900) writer, painter, art critic and reformer, born in London, England expressed himself in the following way about success: **"THE HIGHEST REWARD FOR MAN'S TOIL IS NOT WHAT HE GETS FOR IT, BUT WHAT HE BECOMES BY IT."**

Finally, we must understand that if we have confidence in ourselves and we are sure that we deserve to succeed, we will do everything impossible and unimaginably necessary to achieve it. Otherwise, we ourselves will be boycotting ourselves. Many times we do not achieve what we want because in reality we are not convinced, and we do not clearly know what we want nor do we know what we must do to achieve it. It is clear that success must apply to our daily lives, because as someone said: "**SUCCESS IS A JOURNEY, NOT A DESTINATION.**"

Here are some quotes from men who excelled in life, so that they can also help you on this journey called success.

As Michael John Bobak, digital artist and best known for this quote, said: "**ALL PROGRESS TAKES PLACE OUTSIDE THE COMFORT ZONE.**"

One of the successful quotes by Swami Vivekananda (1863-1902), Indian religious and spiritual leader propagating the Hindu doctrines of Vedanta and Yoga is: "**MAKE THAT ONE IDEA YOUR**

LIFE- THINK OF IT, DREAM OF IT, LIVE ON THAT IDEA. LET THE BRAIN, MUSCLES, NERVES, EVERY PART OF YOUR BODY BE FULL WITH THAT IDEA AND, JUST LEAVE EVERY OTHER IDEA ALONE. THIS IS THE WAY TO SUCCESS."

A hit phrase that describes the steps to success of the great vecturing manufacturer Henry Ford: **"COMING TOGETHER IS A BEGINNING; KEEPING TOGETHER IS PROGRESS; WORKING TOGETHER IS SUCCESS."**

It may take a bit of time, just like Disney, but if you stay on track it's going to deliver. From Walt Disney: **"ALL OUR DREAMS CAN COME TRUE, IF WE HAVE THE COURAGE TO PURSUE THEM."**

There is no need to despair if you do not have incredible qualities, Bruce Lee affirmed: **"THE SUCCESSFUL WARRIOR IS THE AVERAGE MAN, WITH LASER-LIKE FOCUS."**

This phrase by Jim Rohn invites us to order our priorities: **"IF YOU ARE NOT WILLING TO RISK THE UNUSUAL, YOU WILL HAVE TO SETTLE FOR THE ORDINARY."**

ELEVENTH PART

THE POWER OF LEADERSHIP

"The speed of the Leader determines the pace of the pack." Unknown author

Leadership is the **ability of an individual (Leader)** to exercise with their example on the members of their organization and enthuse them to work in a positive way to achieve the common goal.

Johann Wolfgang von Goethe was a German poet, playwright and scientist who was born in Frankfurt (1749-1832), and stated in one of his writings: "**A GREAT PERSON ATTRACTS GREAT PEOPLE AND KNOWS HOW TO KEEP THEM TOGETHER.**"

As we said, a leader is the person who, through their example, marks the way forward. If their thoughts and actions are small, their achievements will be small, and their great thoughts put into practice will become great works.

What are you doing to make your Leadership really great, interesting and productive? For this reason, as a good Leader, you must choose and train capable people to do the job, controlling them sufficiently, but without interfering while they are doing it.

A true Leader must be: Committed, Active, Self motivated, Loyal, Responsible and Organized. Only then will you become a champion and be able to do a little more than what others do.

A leader is agile in their thoughts, actions and planning. Their agility determines the speed of the team. In other words, a leader is a man or woman who knows where he or she is going. Without hesitation, they confidently go towards the goal they set for themselves. Things are great because we make them great! Leaders plan their team of Advisors' work without departing from company policy. They know how to set goals for their organization and evaluate the overall results of the organization and particular of the Consultants.

Some of their specific functions include:

1.- Hire and train the new Advisor.

2.- Make sure that the New and Active Advisors have a very good knowledge of the process or services they sell.

3.- Help the Advisors in defining the goals and establishing the group goal.

4.- Supervise the work of the Advisors by means of communication, telephone calls, emails and meetings.

5.- Must suggest new sales programs and intervene in company decisions related to sales policy.

6.- Design and present sales strategies and reports so that company managers can analyze them.

7.- Attend seminars to increase your preparation as a Leader, and hold conferences with the Advisors of your organization.

8.- Have the ability to resolve problems, complaints or queries that arise related to your sales organization.

Billionaire Richard Charles Nocholas Branson was born on July 18, 1950, in Blackheath, United Kingdom. He was a successful entrepreneur known for forming the Virgin brand, which has a network of

more than 360 companies, and this is how he pronounced himself with respect to Leaders: "**A GOOD LEADER DOES NOT GET STUCK BEHIND A DESK.**"The figure of the Leader is very important for a company to achieve commercial objectives. Unfortunately, many times the Leader does not have the skills to perform in such a delicate and important position. To occupy a Leadership position, the subject must have many skills that allow, not only to increase sales, but also to have the ability to know how to organize a work team. These competencies are:

Control the activities of your group: Generally, we think that in the sales department what counts are the productions; this is a half truth. The Leader must take into account not only the productions, but must also look beyond the present, analyze the ethics of their Advisors as well as the loyalty of the clients and their satisfaction with the products and services they acquired.

Ability to attract and Develop new Advisors: The Leader must have the ability to attract new members to his or her sales group.

Ability in the art of Motivation: In sales there are moments of negativity when the results are not what was expected. It is precisely in those moments when the Leader must have the ability to motivate himself or herself to move forward without being discouraged, and mainly the ability to motivate his or her sales organization so that despair does not crumble it.

Being a Good Negotiator: The Leader is responsible for negotiating with the company directors about the sales policy. For this reason, he or she must have the necessary negotiation skills and the ability to negotiate with his or her sales team on the importance of complying the corporate goal.

Good Communication: As a Leader you must not only have the ability to motivate your organization, but also the ability to communicate with them without ambiguity and without creating discontent in the group.

Know the operation of the Company: It is essential that the Leader have a deep knowledge of the organization and the financial strength of the company, in this way he or she can set real goals for his or her group that adapt to the situation of the company.

Klaus Balkenhol is a German equestrian and Olympic champion who won a gold medal in team dressage at the 1992 Summer Olympics in Barcelona, and thus referred to the Leader: **"THERE IS A DIFFERENCE BETWEEN BEING A LEADER AND BEING A BOSS. BOTH ARE BASED ON AUTHORITY. A BOSS DEMANDS BLIND OBEDIENCE; A LEADER EARNS HIS AUTHORITY THROUGH UNDERSTANDING AND TRUST."** This position associated with power but in turn responsibility and commitment, can become a heavy burden for the Leader.

In this sense, this is how the great Greek philosopher Aristotle pronounced himself: **"HE WHO HAS NEVER LEARNED TO OBEY CANNOT BE A GOOD COMMANDER."** Leading is not easy: you have to assume the direction that the team takes, face the difficulties both in the task and among the members of the group or the consequences and responsibilities that derive from the decisions that are made.

1.- The most successful leaders are those who recognize the creative potential of each of the people who work with them and use it productively.

2.- A company has literally thousands of potential leaders. All they need is self-realization and self-motivation to fulfill their destiny.

3.- A good leader is not restricted by the way things have always been done. His or her leadership is a continuous search to find the best way, not the best known.

4-. The person who motivates himself or herself to be a leader has the time and capacity to overcome their fears.

5.- The most effective leadership is exercised by example.

6.- All leaders who achieve success have an attitude that attracts them, they have habits that promote, they know where they stand and where they are going. To guide oneself is the most important quality of leadership.

7.- To lead others you have to start with yourself. If the price of leadership is to be paid, we will surely have to accept that condition.

8.- The mark that distinguishes a true leader is knowing how to make decisions.

9.- Raising the image of the company and its executives will improve its presence in the market - because everyone likes to work in a large company-, as well as assuming greater responsibility in the recruitment and training of its personnel. Finally, provide better services to clients and Advisors.

10.- Put into practice the elaborated plan, without allowing anything and anybody to distract you from carrying it out.

11.- Transform the goal for results.

12.- Do not believe you are essential, that you must do everything, do not try so hard to do it, share the responsibilities.

13.- You must have a project to carry out the work, if you do not have a program you will think that you are never moving forward.

14.- You must like your work, otherwise, if you do not change your attitude towards your work, this will become a burden. It is better that you change your attitude towards your job or change jobs.

15.- Do not think that you can do it all at once, do one thing at a time. Example: if you are in the savannah and you are hungry, and you get a freshly killed elephant, can you satisfy your hunger? You can't swallow it whole - you can't - but you can eat it bite by bite. This is life, you have to live it day by day.

16.- Approach your work with the correct Mental Attitude. If you think it is boring and difficult that's the way it will be; if instead you see it as easy and fun it will be this way.

17.- With competence and efficiency it will always be easier to carry out your activity.

18.- Stay calm and do it calmly so you can do it easily.

19.- Discipline is extremely important. Don't put off for tomorrow what you can do today.

Try using these methods and you will see how your tasks will be accomplished more easily and quickly.

In all world organizations, Leaders are, first of all, change agents. They are people whose decisions and actions affect other people, in the sense that they positively or negatively modify their attitudes to achieve common goals.

John Peter Zenger (1697-1746) was a German printer and journalist in New York City. He was a great critic of the English colonial system and had many problems with the justice system. When asked about the characteristics of a good Leader, he replied: "**GREAT LEADERS ARE NOT DEFINED BY THE ABSENCE OF WEAKNESS, BUT RATHER BY THE PRESENCE OF CLEAR STRENGTHS.**"

The business world and decision making are increasingly dynamic, which is why the emotional coefficient becomes more important than just intellectual capacity. Today it has been shown that emotional intelligence is a very important element in the performance in the life of the human being and the decisions that are taken. Douglas Mac Arthur (1880-1964) was a five-star general in the United States Army and a field marshal in the Philippine Army; he also served as Supreme Allied Commander on the Pacific Front during World War II. He is the most decorated military man in the history of the United States of America, and he affirmed that a Leader is not made, but becomes one automatically by his or her abilities: **"A TRUE LEADER HAS THE CONFIDENCE TO STAND ALONE, THE COURAGE TO MAKE TOUGH DECISIONS, AND THE COMPASSION TO LISTEN TO THE NEEDS OF OTHERS. HE DOES NOT SET OUT TO BE A LEADER, BUT BECOMES ONE BY THE EQUALITY HIS ACTIONS AND THE INTEGRITY OF HIS INTENT."**

An ingredient of Albert Schweitzer's Leadership is to serve as an example; this makes someone recognized and worthy of respect, and even leadership, and affirms: **"EXAMPLE IS NOT THE MAIN THING IN INFLUENCING OTHERS. IT IS THE ONLY THING."**

In addition, a Leader must be a Professional Advisor:

1.- Understand the client and their needs.

2.- Know the business, the products, the sales process, the tools, the company's policies and the environment.

3.- Propose solutions that support the client without harming the Company.

4.- They are allies of our organization and they fight to achieve the goals.

5.- They continuously advise our clients with constant service visits.

A leader must be optimistic:

1.- Leaders are convinced that the corporative goal has to be and must be reached.

2.- Motivate their organization to reach their goals on behalf of everyone's interest.

3.- Obstacles are not an impediment; they find an opportunity in each one of them.

4.- They set goals and strive to reach them.

5.- Their optimism propels them to develop and be flexible.

Leaders promote change and transformation of the business:

1.- Understand our Advisers' needs, clients and the company's, and adapt to each situation.

2.- Check and modify their way of thinking and acting on a daily basis.

3.- Agility in decision making and supporting them.

Leaders maintain trustworthy relationships:

1.- Value the differences and develop in the midst of diversity.

2.- Generate credibility through consistency in their behaviour.

3.- Act according to the company's ethics.

4.- Work convinced that by helping others in attaining their goals theirs are achieved.

Leaders have excellent performance:

1.- Always maintain excellent behavior, know how to self-evaluate the activity and work to exceed the goal.

2.- They promote excellence at all levels.

3.- They like challenges, and they feel proud of overcoming obstacles.

4.- They seek to carry out the best business for the benefit of the organization.

Leaders have an avant-garde vision:

1-. Implement novel changes.

2-. They always anticipate situations with a Positive Mental Attitude.

3-. They identify transcendent opportunities and projects

4-. To improve the quality of your organization it is necessary to break all the paradigms of the past. Today the world and its people are completely different, so we must not resist changes.

5-. Therefore, one must replace rigidity with flexibility, verticality with horizontality, an open and positive attitude, in short, a lot of elasticity with firmness in one's leadership.

6-. Leaders must assume that our clients are much more intelligent and demanding than in the past, therefore this must be the basis to be able to train our Advisors the best way possible to be successful, and thus strengthen our organization. For this reason, it is necessary to maintain an open mind and a strong Positive Mental Attitude and be receptive to the technological development that is generated, to apply them in the sales processes.

7-. Your theoretical knowledge and your experience as a Leader must match what your Advisors do in the field of sale. This is achieved through exemplary leadership, always with innovative criteria. The experience plus the theoretical knowledge is important to improve the quality of the training, thus increasing the productivity of the organization and at the same time increasing the knowledge of its Advisors, preparing them to occupy leadership positions in the future.

What is Coaching?

1-. Coaching is an integrated set of actions aimed at improving the performance of salespeople, so that they can reach their production potential.

2-. In sales organizations, coaching is a systematic form of training usually conducted by an outside professional, a co-worker, or by the person's supervisor.

3-. Generally, coaching seeks to build skills such as communication, problem solving, teamwork, or sales. It is also frequently used to enhance personal characteristics such as impact or assertiveness.

However, coaching is not something that is practiced by many in our organizations, for this reason it is important to include these elements:

1-. Communicate to your new Advisors what the company expects of them.

2-. Trust the judgment of your people.

3-. Assign necessary responsibilities to your collaborators.

4-. Demonstrate confidence in others by recognizing the abilities to achieve objectives.

5-. Publicly reward those who excel at work. This motivates others to stand out.

6-. Accept and support the suggestions of others.

7-. Value the capacity of others in the performance of their position, in this way they are developing new leaders.

8-. Accept mistakes without criticizing them, and guide continuous improvement. Therefore, as the Leader of your organization you must continually evaluate your Advisors and develop systems that help you improve productivity.

9-. It is important to develop emotional intelligence in your Advisors and thus learn skills of self-knowledge, self-control, motivation, etc. It is important for your growth and that of your organization.

10-. The Leader must be able to plan a common goal motivating all the Advisors to embrace it.

Finally, the Leader should, through motivation, be able to enable Advisors to achieve it effectively.

11-. The Leader is not afraid that someone in their organization will not agree on some decisions and that they can freely express themselves on the criteria of organizing the team. On the contrary, you should encourage free discussion to improve the procedures of the sales policy and have the courage to adopt new ideas for the common good, in this way you are involving everyone in achieving the goal of the group.

The Great Napoleon Bonaparte is said to have said the following phrase in front of his soldiers: "**All soldiers in the French army are potentially marshals.**" This phrase was interpreted as a motivation for all the soldiers. But this same phrase can be transferred to any organization, for example, in sales we say that: "the best Leader has not yet entered, it could be you." The only thing he lacks is confidence, a lot of faith and mainly an unwavering Positive Mental Attitude.

One of the biggest lies is that most people believe that to be a Leader you have to be born with the relative qualities to hold the position, THIS IS A LIE! We can all learn to be Leaders, all we have to do is want it intensely.

If a Leader pressures or manipulates their team to achieve the goal, surely the results will be the worst and they will never reach the desired goal. The Positive Leader understands that their organization must be motivated and that each individual feel important. It is the one that continually motivates the Advisors of your organization as a group or separately, making them see how important it is to achieve the corporate goal and what would be the dividends they could receive.

Similarly, the Leader must worry about the necessary training of his or her team and the formation of new Leaders. They do not realize the great added value that both the company and its organization receive to develop other leaders. Ultimately, the

Leader must ensure that his or her group is compact and well-formed so that they can meet common goals.In conclusion, undoubtedly being a Leader is

not an easy task, but it is not impossible either. Anyone with a lot of confidence, faith, enthusiasm and a Positive Mental A   ttitude   can   achieve leadership. I want to finish with a phrase that I used previously: **"THE BEST LEADER HAS NOT YET JOINED THE COMPANY, IT COULD BE YOU."**

TWELFTH PART

IN SEARCH OF EXCELLENCE

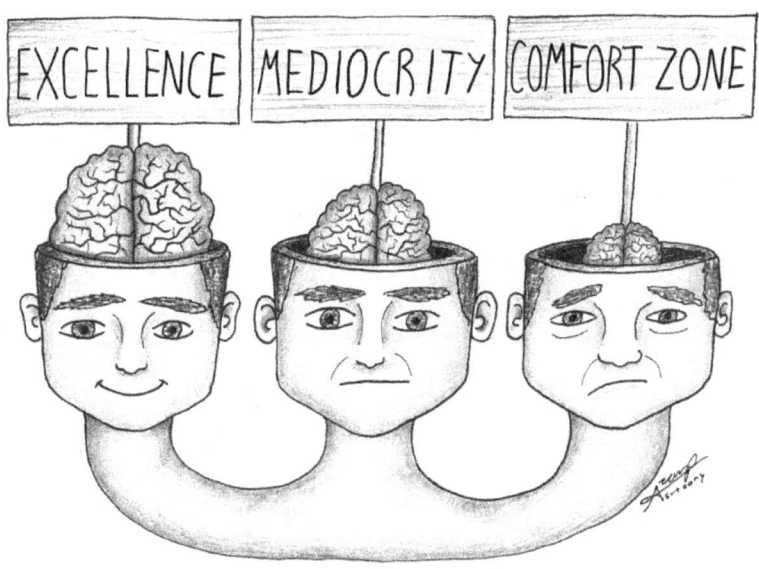

"Do you know great minds enjoy
excellence, average minds love
mediocrity and small minds adore
comfort zones?"

-Onyi Anyado

Excellence is a word that comes from the Latin *excellentia*, which highlights the qualities that an individual possesses by defining oneself as excellent. To be excellent you must perform all your tasks perfectly and not look for excuses as to why they were not done. To really enjoy our profession with satisfaction, we must do it with extreme excellence. Actually, an excellent attitude at work not only yields good results, it is also highly satisfactory for those who practice it.

As we seek excellence, we will stay younger because it forces us to be more active. All women and men, through excellence, can always improve both in their personal life and in their professional activity.

Being excellent forces us to be more upright and increases our passion to feel truly different. Seeking excellence implies acting with excellence, always giving your best. Even when excellence is perceived as distant, it is the interest and effort that we make to achieve excellence that has the most value, just by the simple fact of wanting and acting to achieve excellence brings us closer to the end result: being excellent.

You need to develop a strong discipline, which will allow you to forge the personality of an achiever, that will transform you into excellent and therefore, to success. Ultimately, excellence turns out to be an exercise in intelligence and patience, which once achieved will highly reward those who had enough perseverance to overcome all difficulties.

From a very young age, the Greek philosopher Aristotle (384-322 BC) was instructed by his father in the secrets of medicine, fueling his passion for experimental research years later. This is how he defined excellence: **"WE ARE WHAT WE REPEATEDLY DO. EXCELLENCE THEN, IS NOT AN ACT, BUT A HABIT."**

If we want to live a bright and exciting life, we must constantly seek excellence. This way of acting will make the people around us admire us. Everyone should strive to improve in all personal and professional activities in their life. The important thing is that you dedicate yourself to some activity and do it with excellence. If you always act with excellence, you will see the wonderful change in your life. To be an excellent person in any profession, you must be willing to make a number of sacrifices that most people do not want to make.

James Franklin Murphy is an American guitarist who used to say this about excellence: **"SEEKING**

EXCELLENCE MEANS CHOOSING TO FORGE YOUR OWN SWORD TO CUT THROUGH THE LIMITATIONS OF YOUR LIFE."

Excellence is surpassing yourself and rising higher than the average person. Unfortunately, many people settle for mediocrity; you cannot afford to be mediocre, you must overcome this by rejecting the idea of doing only what allows you to survive.

All of us were created in the image and likeness of our Creator, who without a doubt created us to be achievers in our lives. Be an excellent Advisor and you will inevitably be a winner.

The Greek philosopher Aristotle always stated: "EXCELLENCE IS AN ART WON BY TRAINING AND HABITUATION. WE DO NOT ACT RIGHTLY BECAUSE WE HAVE VIRTUE OR EXCELLENCE, BUT WE RATHER HAVE THOSE BECAUSE WE HAVE ACTED RIGHTLY. WE ARE

WHAT WE REPEATEDLY DO. EXCELLENCE, THEN, IS NOT AN ACT BUT A HABIT."

As an excellent person you must have clear goals, developing an action plan to achieve them and launching yourself without fear to reach them. Do not worry about the obstacles that will appear only when you stop concentrating on the goal. Try to always surpass the best. Doing extraordinary things - an extra in everything you do - will then make everything extraordinarily excellent.

Arnaldo Calveyra, Argentine philosopher and writer who received the Diploma of Merit from the Konex award in 2014 explains what excellence is: **"YOU HAVE TO WALK UP AND KNOCK ON EXCELLENCE'S DOOR BECAUSE IT IS A SEVEN DAY A WEEK JOB."**

Today the world is completely different and people are more professionally prepared. This requires greater virtues to be a man of excellence. Erase all of the ideas of failure and impossibilities from your thoughts, because anything is possible! The difference between success and failure is knowing how to recognize the opportunity. You will constantly find yourself facing great opportunities that seem more like problems without solutions.

Finally, as the great Henry Ford, inventor of the assembly line in the automotive industry, said: **"FAILURE IS SIMPLY THE OPPORTUNITY TO BEGIN AGAIN, THIS TIME MORE INTELLIGENTLY**." Remember that by getting up after failure you will certainly succeed. Only you are responsible for your life.

1. Being excellent is doing things, not looking for reasons to show that they cannot be done.

2. Being excellent is understanding that life is not something that is given to us, but that we have to produce opportunities to achieve success.

3. Being excellent is understanding that with a strong discipline it is possible to forge a character of success.

4.Being excellent is making a plan for yourself and achieving your desired goals despite all of the circumstances.

5. Being excellent is knowing how to say "I was wrong"and trying not to make the same mistake.

6.Being excellent is getting up every time you fail with a spirit of learning and improvement.

7. Being excellent is understanding that through the daily privilege of our work we can achieve fulfillment.

8. To be excellent is to demand of ourselves the full development of our potentialities, tirelessly seeking fulfillment.

9. Being excellent is exercising our freedom and being responsible for each one of our actions.

10. To be excellent is to create something: a system, a position, a company, a home and a life.

11. To be excellent is to feel upset and take action against poverty, slander and injustice.

12. Being excellent is closing your eyes and dreaming of achieving the impossible.

13. To be excellent is to transcend our time, leaving a better world to the future generations.

Although most accept what others do, do not accept it. Make an extraordinary effort to transform yourself into an excellent being and thus you can have a satisfying and happy life. Your effort will be rewarded because it will allow you to live above the mediocre.

John Thomas Grinder was an American Anglicist and linguist best known for being the co-founder, along with Richard Bandler, of the technique called neurolinguistic programming. His suggestion on excellence is as follows: **"IF YOU GO AROUND THE WORLD LOOKING FOR EXCELLENCE, YOU WILL FIND EXCELLENCE; IF YOU GO AROUND THE WORLD LOOKING FOR PROBLEMS, YOU WILL FIND PROBLEMS. OR AS THE ARABIC PROVERB SAYS: WHAT A PIECE OF BREAD CAN MEAN WILL**  **DEPEND ON WHETHER YOU ARE HUNGRY OR NOT."**

THIRTEENTH PART

THE SUCCESSFUL ADVISOR

"Coming together is a beginning;
keeping together is progress;
working together is success."

- Henry Ford.

"IF YOU CAN DREAM IT, YOU CAN DO IT." -Walt Disney. The word triumphant also comes from the Latin *triumphātor* and comes from the verb "triumph" and the suffix "dor". This word refers to the person who does something transcendental.

By definition, the winner is the one who triumphs, destroys, defeats, conquers, dominates, etc., the one who gainsachievements in his or her profession or some other area of their life.

An achiever is simply that Advisor with the Positive Mental Attitude, through which he or she learned to achieve his or her goals regardless of the obstacles that had to be overcome.

Our creators created us to be achievers. You are a winner from birth, that's more than enough to make you feel worthy of success.

You must daily say to yourself: "**I am a winner**". When you are doing something, act and think as if you have already succeeded. Always be optimistic; Positive Mental Attitude and success go together.

The simple fact of acting with a Positive Mental Attitude and thinking like a winner works gradually and favorably on what you think. Confucius, the famous Chinese philosopher said: "**SUCCESS DEPENDS UPON PREVIOUS PREPARATION, AND WITHOUT SUCH PREPARATION THERE IS SURE TO BE FAILURE.**"

The successful Advisor has an unshakable faith, a very firm confidence, both of which give him or her an unassailable enthusiasm and generates a formidable Positive Mental Attitude, which will lead him or her to be optimistic. One will feel good about oneself and it will help the advisor achieve success.

John Ruskin (1819-1900) British writer, art critic and sociologist said: **"WHEN LOVE AND SKILL WORK TOGETHER, EXPECT A MASTERPIECE."**

1. The Advisor who wishes to be an Achiever is committed and will achieve their goals against all odds. The Adviser is not used to procrastinating and will always keep their promise.

2. For the winner there are only challenges. Problems are only opportunities in disguise to achieve success.

3. The Achiever recognizes when he or she has failed. As the great Henry Ford said: **"FAILURE IS SIMPLY THE OPPORTUNITY TO BEGIN AGAIN, THIS TIME MORE INTELLIGENTLY."**

4. The Achiever knows that merit breeds confidence and faith, trust and faith breeds enthusiasm and enthusiasm gives the individual a very excellent Positive Mental Attitude that will allow the Achiever to conquer the world.

William Clement Stone (1902-2002) was an entrepreneur, philanthropist and author of New Thought self-help books and used to say: **"SUCCESS IS ACHIEVED AND MAINTAINED BY THOSE WHO TRY AND KEEP TRYING."** The successful Advisor knows that their work is good, but does not settle for less than success.

5. The Achiever enjoys healthy self-esteem, recognizes values and knows how valuable they are for a company. As some unknown writer said: **"THOSE WHO FEEL SELF-ESTIMATION WILL GET GOOD RESULTS."**

6. The Advisor who succeeds has a confidence of steel and knows that attitude is more important than facts. As Mark Twain said: **"ALL YOU NEED IN THIS LIFE IS IGNORANCE AND CONFIDENCE, AND THEN SUCCESS IS SURE."**

7. The Successful Advisor knows himself and this brings him many and wide benefits, since he will know how to control himself and will act according to the different occasions.

8. The Achievers are simple. Simplicity makes their personality more attractive, showing themselves as they truly are.

Carefully remember that becoming a successful Advisor is not an easy thing; you will not be able to achieve it instantly. It is a change that occurs gradually if you maintain a Positive Mental Attitude. You must be willing to make some changes that are preventing you from reaching your victory. It is important to keep in mind that being a winner has nothing to do with the money you have. Succeeding means fighting to achieve your dreams with ethics and honesty.

The famous scientist Albert Einstein (1879-1955) developed the theory of relativity, revolutionizing science the way it was known until the 20th century.

One of his famous statements is: **"TRY NOT TO BECOME A MAN OF SUCCESS, BUT RATHER TRY TO BECOME A MAN OF VALUE."**

We can all certainly be achievers. The advisers who are constantly in the first places, those who win all the awards and contests are the most admired for their achievements in our organizations. These are the true winners.

Arnold H. Glasgow (1905-1998) was a famous US businessman. He marketed a humor magazine for companies. On one occasion he defined success this way: **"SUCCESS IS SIMPLE. DO WHAT'S RIGHT, THE RIGHT WAY, AT THE RIGHT TIME."**

To end this book, I want to leave you with some quotes from celebrities who have succeeded in their lives.

"SUCCESS LIES IN FEELING SATISFACTION WHEN YOU GIVE MORE THAN YOU HAVE." - Christopher Reeve, (1952-2004) American actor who gained worldwide fame after portraying the mythical superhero Superman in 1978.

"IN ORDER TO ATTAIN THE IMPOSSIBLE, ONE MUST ATTEMPT THE ABSURD." - Miguel de Cervantes. (1508-1616) famous for his work Don Quixote de la Mancha.

"YOU DON'T HAVE TO BE A GENIUS OR A VISIONARY OR EVEN A COLLEGE GRADUATE TO BE SUCCESSFUL. YOU JUST NEED A FRAMEWORK AND A DREAM." -

Michael Saul Dell (1965) is a businessman, investor and philanthropist from the United States. He is the founder and CEO of Dell Inc., one of the leading computer vendors in the world.

"THERE ARE THREE TYPES OF PEOPLE: THERE ARE PEOPLE WHO MAKE THINGS HAPPEN, THERE ARE PEOPLE WHO WATCH THINGS HAPPEN, AND THERE ARE PEOPLE WHO WONDER WHAT HAPPENED. TO BE SUCCESSFUL, YOU NEED TO BE A PERSON WHO MAKES THINGS HAPPEN." - James Arthur Lovell Jr. (1928), known as Jim Lovell, former American NASA astronaut and retired captain of the United States Navy, known for being the commander of the Apollo 13 mission, which suffered a critical failure on the trip to the Moon, but was brought back safely to Earth thanks to the efforts of the crew and mission control.

"THE SIZE OF YOUR SUCCESS IS MEASURED BY THE STRENGTH OF YOUR DESIRE; THE SIZE OF YOUR DREAMS; AND HOW YOU HANDLE DISAPPOINTMENT ALONG THE WAY." - Robert Kiyosaki (Robert Toru Kiyosaki) is a Hawaiian businessman of Japanese descent born in 1947. He writes financial self-help books and is a renowned motivational speaker, well known for his famous book "Rich Dad Poor Dad."

YOU DECIDE WHICH GROUP YOU WANT TO BELONG TO.

SUCCESS

SUCCESS

SUCCESS

Acknowledgements

I want to thank the following people: my daughter Arianna Coltellacci, because she motivated and encouraged me to write this book. Pablo Azar and Ana Carolina Grajales (Toonymania LLC), for collaborating with the creative management and conceptualization of graphic ideas. Nicoletta Giannini for proofreading and correction of the Italian edition. I wish for all of you to always be very successful in every project you undertake.

I dedicate this book to all of the professional Leaders and Advisors, and to those who want to get started in this fantastic profession called sales.

OTHER BOOKS

YOU MAY ALSO LIKE

Available on Amazon